Fifties

The Fun Years!

Jim Chumley

summersdale

FIFTIES: THE FUN YEARS!

Copyright © Summersdale Publishers Ltd, 2011

Illustrations by John Lightbourne

Summersdale Publishers Ltd
46 West Street
Chichester
West Sussex
PO19 1RP
UK

www.summersdale.com

Printed and bound in China

ISBN: 978-1-84953-115-3

Substantial discounts on bulk quantities of Summersdale books are available to corporations, professional associations and other organisations. For details contact Summersdale Publishers by telephone: +44 (0) 1243 771107, fax: +44 (0) 1243 786300 or email: nicky@summersdale.com.

To...

From..

We're vintage!

Jennifer Saunders and Dawn French
on both reaching fifty

They say that age is all in your mind. The trick is keeping it from creeping down into your body.

Anonymous

I refuse to admit that I am more than fifty-two, even if that makes my children illegitimate.

Nancy Astor

Don't just count your years, make your years count.

George Meredith

Cherish forever what makes you
unique, 'cuz you're really a yawn
if it goes.

Bette Midler

I'm officially middle-aged. I don't need drugs any more, thank God. I can get the same effect just by standing up real fast.

Jonathan Katz

Years may wrinkle the skin, but to give up enthusiasm wrinkles the soul.

Samuel Ullman

Getting old is a fascinating
thing. The older you get,
the older you want to get.

Keith Richards

I finally figured out the only reason to be
alive is to enjoy it.

Rita Mae Brown

There's a kind of confidence that comes when you're in your forties and fifties, and men find that incredibly attractive.

Peggy Northrop

I'm limitless as far as age is concerned... as long as he has a driver's licence.

Kim Cattrall on dating younger men

I'm surprised that I'm fifty... I still feel like a kid.

Bruce Willis

The first sign of maturity is the discovery that the volume knob also turns to the left.

Jerry M. Wright

Middle age is when a guy keeps turning off lights for economical rather than romantic reasons.

Eli Cass

Years ago we discovered the exact point, the dead centre of middle age. It occurs when you are too young to take up golf and too old to rush to the net.

Franklin Adams

People who say you're
just as old as you feel are
all wrong, fortunately.

Russell Baker

We are always the same age inside.

Gertrude Stein

Age does not protect you from love.
But love to some extent, protects you
from age.

Jeanne Moreau

I feel stronger now than, maybe, twenty years ago. If your mind is strong, your body will be strong.

Madonna

You know you're getting old when all
the names in your black book have
MD after them.

Harrison Ford

The other day a man asked me what
I thought was the best time of life.
'Why,' I answered without a
thought, 'now.'

David Grayson

Old wood best to burn, old wine to drink, old friends to trust, and old authors to read.

Francis Bacon

To get back my youth I would do anything in the world; except take exercise, get up early, or be respectable.

Oscar Wilde

The really frightening thing about middle age is that you know you'll grow out of it!

Doris Day

There is only one cure for grey hair.
It was invented by a Frenchman. It is
called the guillotine.

P. G. Wodehouse

Only the middle-aged have
all their five senses in the
keeping of their wits.

Hervey Allen

The young sow wild oats. The old
grow sage.

Winston Churchill

Wisdom doesn't necessarily come with age. Sometimes age just shows up all by itself.

Tom Wilson

Forty is the old age of youth; fifty is
the youth of old age.

Victor Hugo

40   **50**

Be kind to your kids, they'll be choosing your nursing home.

Anonymous

Inflation is when you pay fifteen dollars for the ten-dollar haircut you used to get for five dollars when you had hair.

Sam Ewing

When young we are faithful to
individuals, when older we grow loyal
to situations and to types.

Cyril Connolly

The first forty years of life give us the text; the next thirty supply the commentary on it.

Arthur Schopenhauer

You know you're getting old when you stop to tie your shoes and wonder what else you can do while you're down there.

George Burns

There are only three ages for women in Hollywood: *Babe, District Attorney,* and *Driving Miss Daisy.*

Goldie Hawn

I look forward to being older, when what you look like becomes less and less an issue and what you are is the point.

Susan Sarandon

I have enjoyed greatly the second blooming... suddenly you find – at the age of fifty, say – that a whole new life has opened before you.

Agatha Christie

The more you praise and celebrate
your life, the more there is in life
to celebrate.

Oprah Winfrey

No matter how old you are, there's always something good to look forward to.

Lynn Johnston

I'm fifty-six and still
a Virgo.

Liz Carpenter

You're never too old to become younger.

Mae West

I'm not afraid of ageing... I just think: 'Hey, I might as well just go with it.'

Sharon Stone

A diplomat is a man who always
remembers a woman's birthday but
never remembers her age.

Robert Frost

Birthdays only come once a year
unless you're Joan Collins, in which
case they only come every four years.

Steve Bauer

Let us respect grey hairs, especially our own.

J. P. Sears

A man is a fool if he drinks before he reaches fifty, and a fool if he doesn't drink afterward.

Frank Lloyd Wright

When you are younger you get blamed for crimes you never committed and when you're older you begin to get credit for virtues you never possessed. It evens itself out.

I. F. Stone

At age fifty, everyone has the face
he deserves.

George Orwell

To me, fair friend,
you never can be old,
For as you were
when first your eye I eye'd,
Such seems your beauty still.

William Shakespeare, 'Sonnet 104'

At fifty, you know a lot more than you did when you were twenty-five... so you can use all that stuff you didn't know to propel yourself forward.

Oprah Winfrey

I'm aiming by the time I'm
fifty to stop being
an adolescent.

Wendy Cope

It's important to have a twinkle
in your wrinkle.

Anonymous

We've both hit fifty, and we celebrate
it. There is no doomy side to it...
We're nearly grown-up now,
but not quite.

Dawn French and Jennifer Saunders

Few women admit their age. Few men act theirs.

Anonymous

It is not how old you are, but how you are old.

Marie Dressler

Nature gives you the face you have at twenty, but it's up to you to merit the face you have at fifty.

Coco Chanel

I don't believe in ageing. I believe in forever altering one's aspect to the sun. Hence my optimism.

Virginia Woolf

I am not young enough to
know everything.

Oscar Wilde

Youth would be an ideal state if it came a little later in life.

Herbert Henry Asquith

Only the wisest and stupidest of men never change.

Confucius

Fifty is a nice number for the states in the union or for a national speed limit, but it is not a number that I was prepared to have hung on me.

Bill Cosby

Where there is age there is evolution,
where there is life there is growth.

Anjelica Huston

One of the many things nobody ever tells you about middle age is that it's such a nice change from being young.

William Feather

When grace is joined with wrinkles,
it is adorable.

Victor Hugo

Here's a time when you have to
separate yourself from what other
people expect of you, and do
what you love.

Jim Carrey

No wise man ever wished
to be younger.

Jonathan Swift

If you think hitting forty is liberating,
wait till you hit fifty.

Michelle Pfeiffer

Age is just a number. It's totally
irrelevant unless, of course, you
happen to be a bottle of wine.

Joan Collins

Middle age is when your age starts to show around your middle.

Bob Hope

I'm at the age where food has taken the place of sex in my life. In fact, I've just had a mirror put over my kitchen table.

Rodney Dangerfield

Youth is when you're allowed to stay up late on New Year's Eve. Middle age is when you're forced to.

Bill Vaughan

Middle age is youth without levity, and age without decay.

Daniel Defoe

I'm like old wine. They don't bring me out very often, but I'm well preserved.

Rose Kennedy

Age does not diminish the extreme disappointment of having a scoop of ice cream fall from the cone.

Jim Fiebig

The man who views the world at fifty the same as he did at twenty has wasted thirty years of his life.

Muhammad Ali

You take all of the experience and judgment of men over fifty out of the world and there wouldn't be enough left to run it.

Henry Ford

The older you get, the more important
it is not to act your age.

Ashleigh Brilliant

By the time we hit fifty...
we have learned to take life
seriously, but never ourselves.

Marie Dressler

It takes a long time to become young.

Pablo Picasso

You can only perceive real beauty in a person as they get older.

Anouk Aimée

The years between fifty and seventy are the hardest. You are always asked to do things, and you are not yet decrepit enough to turn them down.

T. S. Eliot

As for me, except for an occasional heart attack, I feel as young as I ever did.

Robert Benchley

I'm at an age when my back goes out more than I do.

Phyllis Diller

Wrinkles should merely indicate where
smiles have been.

Mark Twain

Age ain't nothing but a number, so
I feel good.

Denzel Washington

Birthdays are nature's way of telling us
to eat more cake.

Jo Brand

www.summersdale.com